D1252445

BRIGHT
IDEA
BOOKS

CREEPY
URBAN
Legends

by Blake Hoena

CAPSTONE PRESS
a capstone imprint

Bright Idea Books are published by Capstone Press
1710 Roe Crest Drive, North Mankato, Minnesota 56003
www.mycapstone.com

Library of Congress Cataloging-in-Publication Data
Library of Congress Cataloging-in-Publication Data is available on the Library of Congress website.
ISBN: 978-1-5435-4152-6 (library hardcover)
ISBN: 978-1-5435-4192-2 (eBook PDF)

Editorial Credits
Editor: Alexis Burling
Designer: Becky Daum
Production Specialist: Melissa Martin

Photo Credits
AP Images: Jeff Gentner, 20–21; Shutterstock Images: breakermaximus , 26–27, ChiccoDodiFC, 15, DR Travel Photo and Video, 10–11, iiiphevgeniy, 25, Ivan.P, 12–13, Kiselev Andrey Valerevich, 30–31, Lario Tus, 5, Marv Vandehey, 22–23, Ricardo Reitmeyer, 19, Romolo Tavani, 9, 28, Sarawoot Pengmuan, cover, 16–17, Todd Squires, 6–7

Design Elements: iStockphoto, Red Line Editorial, and Shutterstock Images

TABLE OF CONTENTS

CHAPTER 1

SLENDER Man

A **legend** is a **traditional** story.
It is based on a past event. But there
is no proof the story is true.

Urban legends are similar. But they are more modern. Someone tells a made-up story. They may even post it online. The story spreads. People start to believe it is true. Then it becomes an urban legend.

Slender Man is one example. This character was created in 2009. It started as an Internet **meme**. People posted pictures of him online. He was shown as a tall, thin man. He had no face. He wore a dark suit. He **lurked** in the background. But the photos were not real. They were **altered**.

Since then stories have spread about Slender Man. People say he has tentacle-like arms. Some say he hunts children. Others claim to have seen him. They believe he is real.

In some stories Slender Man has extra-long fingers.

SLENDER MAN'S CREATOR

Eric Knudsen created Slender Man. Knudsen posted images of him on a website.

CHAPTER 2

HANDS IN THE
Cemetery

Cemeteries can be scary places.

One of the creepiest is Goodna

Cemetery. It is in Brisbane, Australia.

Some people claim to
have seen ghostly hands
rise up from the ground
at Goodna Cemetery.

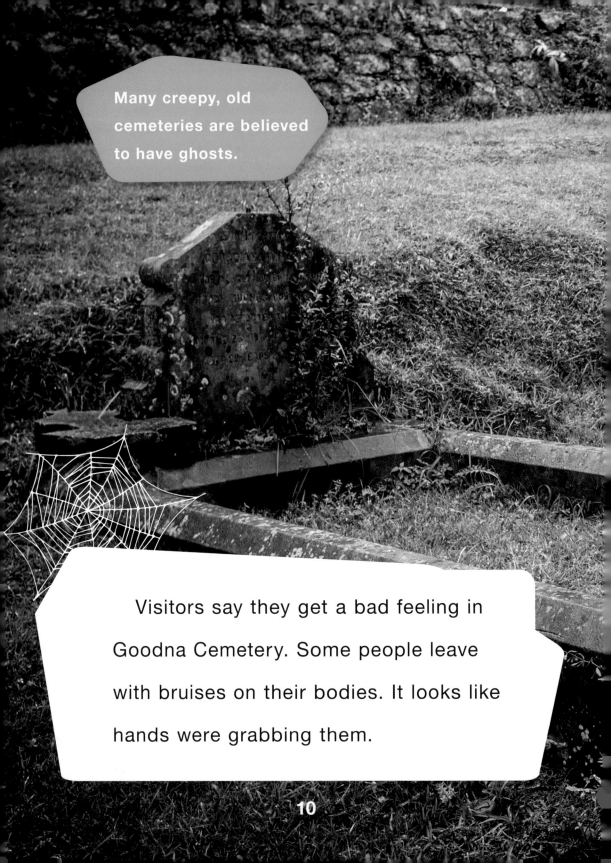

Many creepy, old cemeteries are believed to have ghosts.

Visitors say they get a bad feeling in Goodna Cemetery. Some people leave with bruises on their bodies. It looks like hands were grabbing them.

In one story a man tries to escape the ghostly hands. He jumps into his car. He starts the engine. But the car does not move. He is stuck. He spends the night in his locked car.

Some people claim that long scratches have appeared on cars that stop at the graveyard.

The next morning he gets out.

Deep scratches are all over his car.

It looks like a ghostly creature tried

to get inside.

CHAPTER 3

HANAKO-SAN

Kids often tell stories in school. Sometimes it is to impress their friends. Other times it is to scare them. One of these creepy tales might be the source of Hanako-san. This urban legend started in Japan in the 1950s.

Hanako-san is a ghost. Her spirit is found in school bathrooms. Stories say she **haunts** the third stall. This stall might be out of order. Or it might look unused.

The third stall of a school bathroom may look normal. But some kids believe Hanako-san still haunts it.

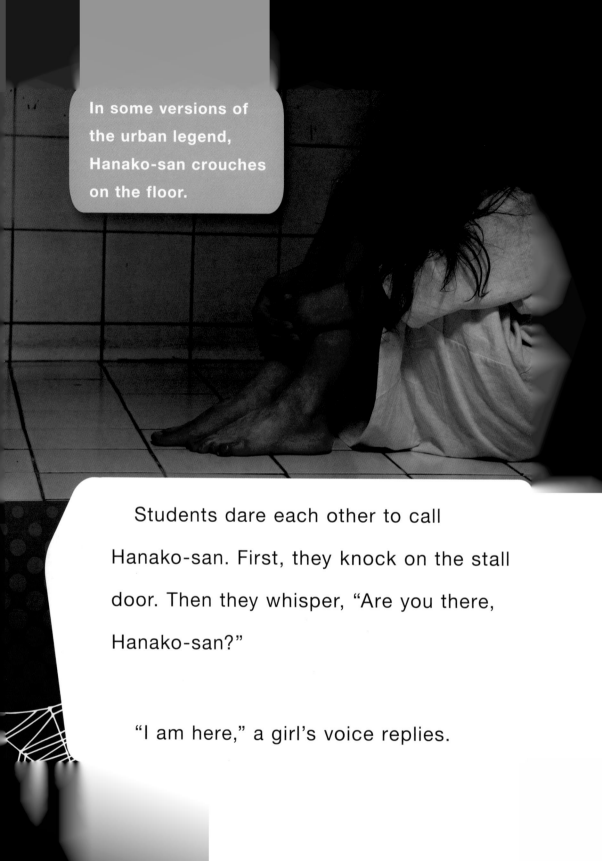

In some versions of the urban legend, Hanako-san crouches on the floor.

Students dare each other to call Hanako-san. First, they knock on the stall door. Then they whisper, "Are you there, Hanako-san?"

"I am here," a girl's voice replies.

Stories vary about what happens next. Some say a ghostly girl is in the stall. If a person opens the door, Hanako-san grabs them. She drags them into the toilet. Then she kills them.

Other stories say a three-headed lizard lives in the stall. This creature uses a girl's voice. It calls people into the stall. Then it eats them.

HAUNTED BATHROOMS

A similar ghost is in the Harry Potter series by J. K. Rowling. Myrtle haunts a bathroom at Hogwarts, a school for wizards.

CHAPTER 4

THE
Mothman

On November 12, 1966, people saw a strange creature. It was near Point Pleasant in West Virginia. A group of men were in a cemetery. They saw a dark figure. It looked like a man. But it flew from tree to tree.

Days later a couple saw the creature.

They said it had red, glowing eyes.

It chased them. They jumped in their

car. Then they sped away. The creature

chased them into town.

Cemeteries are common settings of urban legends. People tell stories of scary creatures hiding in the trees.

Other people in the area saw the creature too. Some thought it was a strange animal. Others said it was an alien or something **supernatural**. They called it "Mothman." It looked like a man with wings.

On January 11, 1967, Mothman was seen flying above the town's bridge. Later that year there was an accident. The bridge collapsed. More than 40 people died.

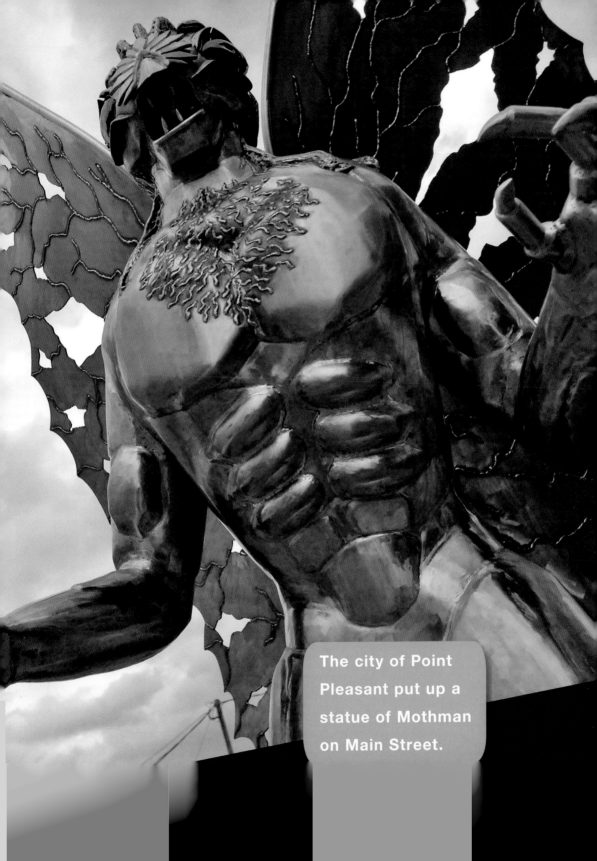

The city of Point Pleasant put up a statue of Mothman on Main Street.

Afterward the Mothman sightings stopped. People said the two events were connected. They believed Mothman was a ghostly creature. It came to warn people about the disaster.

It might be easy to imagine a sandhill crane's brightly colored eyes belong to a supernatural creature instead.

WHAT IS MOTHMAN?

Some people think Mothman was a sandhill crane. This type of bird can have orange or red eyes. It stands several feet tall.

CHAPTER 5

LA MALA HORA

La mala hora means "the bad hour" in Spanish. It is also the name of a creepy ghost. This evil spirit haunts **crossroads** in New Mexico.

In one story a person drives along the road. A black shape leaps in front of the car. The driver slams on the brakes.

It is hard to see *La Mala Hora* when driving at night.

Then there is a screeching sound. A ghostly woman stands next to the car. She has pointed teeth. Her eyes glow red. She claws at the window. The ghost wants to get in the car.

The driver hits the gas and speeds off. When the person gets home, there is a phone call. A loved one has died. *La Mala Hora* came to warn the person about the bad news.

La Mala Hora often wears dark clothing.

GLOSSARY

alter
to change

crossroads
a place where two roads meet

haunt
to visit or appear as a ghost

legend
a historical and often
unbelievable story that cannot
be proven true

lurk
to wait in hiding

meme
an idea or interesting item
that is spread online

supernatural
not able to be explained as a
natural occurrence

traditional
based on the customs of a
group of people

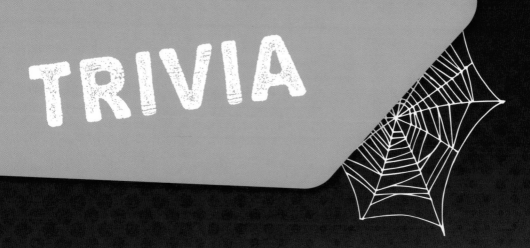

TRIVIA

1. **Woman in White**—Some of the most widely told urban legends are of a woman in a white dress. The woman dies a tragic death. In some urban legends, the woman in white is a sad ghost. In others, she is vengeful and seeks to harm those she meets.

2. **The Candyman**—To summon the Candyman, people turn out the lights in a bathroom. They stare into a mirror and call out his name five times. People believe the Candyman will appear behind them. He is covered in blood and has a hook for a hand.

3. **Vanishing Hitchhiker**—A driver picks up someone along the road. The hitchhiker gets into the back seat. The driver takes the person home. When they arrive, the hitchhiker is gone. The driver finds out the hitchhiker was the ghost of someone who has died.

ACTIVITY

TRY TO DEBUNK AN URBAN LEGEND

All legends are based on something people believe. Pick an urban legend from this book or choose another popular one, such as baby spiders coming out of a spider bite.

First, write down the urban legend. Then circle any facts within the story. Can these facts be proven? Is there evidence to support them? An example would be finding out where spiders really lay their eggs. You may need to do some research.

Next, look at the source behind the urban legend. Who is telling the story? Is it someone who can be trusted? Why, or why not? Also consider explanations. Is there a more believable reason why something happened? An example would be that some people believe the Mothman was actually a sandhill crane because both creatures have similarly colored eyes.

Lastly, write down your conclusion. Why do you think the urban legend is or is not true?

One famous Halloween legend stars a man doomed to wear a jack-o'-lantern on his head.

31

FURTHER RESOURCES

Fascinated by these stories? Read more here:

Cassidy, Tam. *The White Lady Ghost.* New York: PowerKids Press, 2015.

Dyer, Janice. *Haunted Woods and Caves.* New York: Crabtree Publishing Company, 2018.

Peterson, Megan Cooley. *Super Scary Ghosts.* North Mankato, Minn.: Capstone Press, 2017.

Ready to learn more about urban legends? Check out this book:

Kenney, Karen Latchana. *Spine-Tingling Urban Legends.* Minneapolis, Minn.: Lerner Publications, 2017.

INDEX